BREAKTHROUGH

OF

Hope

MY STORY OF HEALING
AFTER ABORTION

SUSAN HUBELE

This is the story of Susan Hubele. What you are about to read is true. However, some names were changed in order to preserve the identities of certain individuals represented in this body of work.

Foreword

I am honored that my friend, Susan, asked me to write a foreword for her powerful book. In *Breakthrough of Hope*, Susan shares her story and wisdom in an open, raw and transparent way just as she does everything in life. I value so much that she shared her experiences without holding anything back knowing the truth would bring freedom to others.

In these pages, Susan tells her story, sharing both the good and bad times, as well as her good and bad choices and the consequences of each. If you or anyone you know has been affected by the tragedy of abortion, you will find the same healing and restoration Susan has experienced by reading her story. You will find redemption and a breakthrough of hope by gleaning from this powerful testimony.

Joe Joe Dawson
Founder and Apostolic Oversight of ROAR Apostolic Network and ROAR Church Texarkana

PISMO BEACH, CALIFORNIA

TABLE OF CONTENTS

· · · · · · · · · ● ● ● ● ● ● ● ● ● ● ● · · · · · ·

May the God of hope fill you with all joy and peace as you trust in Him, so that you may overflow with hope by the power of the Holy Spirit.

Romans 15:13

· · · · · · · · · ● ● ● ● ● ● ● ● ● ● · · · · · · ·

· · · · · · · · · ● ● ● ● ● ● ● ● · · · · · · · · ·

*For I know the thoughts I think toward
you, says the Lord, thoughts of peace
and not of evil, to give you a future and
a hope. And then you will call upon Me
and go and pray to Me, and I will listen
to you. And you will seek me and find
Me, when you search for Me
with all your heart.*

Jeremiah 29:11-13

· · · · · · · · · ● ● ● ● ● ● ● · · · · · · · · ·

A NOTE FROM THE AUTHOR

Most of my life has been a roller coaster ride regarding my walk with the Lord. I have struggled even though I have had excellent teaching and leadership training. However, I just could not shake the turmoil inside of me regarding my past.

How do you heal? How do you truly forgive yourself? How do you overcome the guilt and shame?

For many years I tried to sit and write out my story. It's not one I have told to many people in my life. It is only by God's grace and mercy that I have been set free. Now I am finally able to share my story with you.

As you read what I am about to share with you, I pray you know there is a God who loves you and wants you to be free. I am sharing my story so that you can understand why I am who I am, and all that God has done in me to get me where I am today.

My story is filled with broken pieces, terrible choices and ugly truths. But it is also filled with a major comeback in my soul and a grace that saved my life.

This is my story.

SWINGS AT SANTA BARBARA COUNTY FAIR, SANTA MARIA, CA 1976

Chapter 1

MY YOUNGER YEARS: GROWING UP

I was born in San Diego, California while my dad was on a Navy Aircraft carrier overseas. We moved to the central coast when I was two to a little town called Guadalupe. We lived there until my parents could find a place to live in Santa Maria. Dad started working at Vandenberg Air Force Base , along with many other people in the beginning stages of the Aerospace Industry on the coast. We eventually found a place to live on Pine Street in Santa Maria (this is where I met my very best friend, Linda) and we lived there until I was five. My parents then bought a house in a suburb of Santa Maria called Orcutt, and that is where I did most of my growing up.

We were members of the Methodist church and met many amazing families who were starting their Vandenberg Air Force Base employment. This was an awesome time for me as I made many friends, attended many potlucks at Waller Park, and I got involved with choir and eventually the youth group. At the time,

Mom was involved with a women's group and also did volunteer work.

I was just a normal girl in a middle-class family and had many friends. I lead the average life of a neighborhood girl who enjoyed playing baseball, riding bikes, skateboarding, roller skating down the hills, making forts and climbing trees. I also played with Barbies and other dolls but I was also a little bit of a tom-boy.

I made many great memories with amazing women who were in leadership with both Brownies and Girl Scouts, and I cherish those times growing up. My best friend, Linda, and I had known each other since we were three years old and we were always at her house or my house. We were the best of friends, but really acted more like sisters. We were creative playmates with many shared ideas. One day we invented 'bottomless shoes' out of elastic, buttons and snaps, not realizing that eventually that truly would be a reality for someone else to design and make money on. (You can find them on Pinterest).

Linda and I also loved listening to The Beatles, even as young girls. We played their LP Records, knew all the words to every song, and probably drove our parents crazy! I'm not sure when Linda and her family moved to Three Rivers, but we kept in touch by writing letters to each other through the years. I missed her terribly when we were apart.

In 4th grade, my family and I moved Temporary Duty Yonder to Merritt Island, Florida. My dad's job took him to work at Kennedy Space Center. My dad's regular job at the time was at Vandenberg Air Force Base on the central coast of California. For me living in Florida was scary, but I made several good friends in school. We also went to many neat places for sightseeing. I was able to join up with a local Girl Scout troop where we learned Equestrian riding, and trail riding, which I loved! We were also responsible for taking care of the horses and their stalls. One time we went camping and broke up into different groups, having to name ourselves for each cabin. My group called ourselves, "The Cousin It's". I finished up 4th grade in Florida, and we came back to Orcutt where I started 5th grade.

To this day I have no idea why, but a couple of my friends and I were bullied by other girls starting in 4th grade, including my good friend Audrey, who I'd known since 3rd grade. There were a couple of times girls followed me home from school. They would taunt me, hit me and pull my hair. What was the reason for all of this? Why were they so mean to me?

I learned to hate school and it probably didn't help that I disliked my teacher in 5th grade. It was hard to focus on school subjects and I could tell my teacher was too busy working on his real estate side business during class. Most days I dreaded going to school. The summer before 6th grade, I smoked my first cigarette with one of the popular girls from school. We were goofing off but it made me sick.

I tried smoking here and there, stealing a pack of my dad's cigarettes and getting caught. This was humiliating because my dad tried to make me smoke in front of him. I refused to do it, but when my parents went somewhere, I ended up sneaking out in the backyard to smoke while they were gone.

6th grade came along and I had the most amazing teacher! All of my classmates loved him! He taught us how to read out loud in groups and taught us the most amazing silly songs. He would play his guitar while we all sang together. We also taught us how to Square Dance. He was just an amazing man and a fabulous role model for all of us!

Chapter 2

MY YOUNGER YEARS: JUNIOR HIGH AND HIGH SCHOOL

Junior high came along and I really started hating school and did not care about my grades. I continued to get into trouble here and there, visiting with the school counselor many times while in 7th grade. One time I was suspended because another girl wanted to fight me. I still have no idea why I was the one to be suspended because we never ended up physically fighting.

8th grade was a bit better with no issues for me. I graduated with my class, hoping high school would be better for me to make it through without issues. My Freshman year was from 1972-73. It started out just fine with no issues at first. I made new friends and hoped I would not have any issues with anyone. My friends and I were not popular but we knew many people in the different 'groups' (the Aggies, the dopers, the jocks, the surfers, etc.).

Drill Team tryouts were coming up, and I really wanted to be on the team. I planned on trying out, until some of the girls I went to elementary and junior high school with found out. One day these girls found me in a hallway and pushed me up against a wall, telling me I would NEVER try out for anything. They told me if I were to try out, they would beat me up. I was 5'8" tall and weighed 135 pounds. I wasn't fat or ugly, so why did they hate me so much? Why? What had I really done to make those girls hate me so? Out of fear and intimidation, I never tried out for drill team or anything else.

I didn't have much self-esteem or goals for my life other than to graduate from high school and leave home. I learned to hate the mean girls. Despite everything, I was still a happy go lucky girl, but I was not popular. Writing poetry and reading books became a hobby, and I was pretty good at sewing and crafting. But I still hated school and could not focus on homework because I could not have cared less about my grades.

I was bullied until the 2nd semester of my sophomore year until I stood up for myself. One day I forgot my Geography book and my teacher made me go to my locker to get it. On the way back to class, I ran into one of the mean girls. She threatened to beat me up right there in the hallway. I looked around and asked where her friends were, threw my book down and told her to come on. She walked away.

Wait a minute. What just happened here? I could not believe this girl just walked away after I called her bluff. After that incident, everybody left me alone. I had no idea that all it would take when facing an enemy was to stand up to them.

In high school I ran around with 3 other girls. Of the 4 of us, I was the one who was a little more into the party scene. We all liked to party a bit, but not crazy party. I just liked the thrill of adventure, to party and have a good time goofing off.

Ditching some of my classes was a trend of mine as well. School to me was unimportant with certain classes, but I excelled in others. My GPA was not that great, but I really didn't care. Sometimes on Sunday, my friends and I usually went to Waller Park to play frisbee or drink beer with other people. Lots of people came out to the park to 'cruise' and hang out. One weekend a bunch of people with different vans came out to cruise and show their vehicles. There were so many of them and they each looked amazing inside and out!

My friends and I also liked to go to Avila Beach or Pismo Beach to lay out, play frisbee or body surf. We liked watching the surfers out on the waves, but we never tried to surf. We just body surfed and laid out to get tan. I loved being at the beach, soaking up the rays and being with my friends.

There were times before we went to Avila Beach that we would head up to San Luis Obispo to goof off, see how other people dressed, or just to walk up and down the streets to look at the different shops. On the way to the beach, we would sometimes stop at Madonna Inn to get a piece of pie and look around in the gift shop. Other times we would stop in Shell Beach on our way home to get a burger or stop in Nipomo to get an ice cream cone. We'd also ride our 10-speed bikes on different adventures as well.

Thursday nights in San Luis Obispo were cruise nights, and sometimes we would go up there to join in and meet people. We also hit the cruise on Friday nights in Santa Maria. The cruise in Santa Maria consisted of driving from Jack in The Box to the Taco Bell on the north end of town and then turn around. (Gas was only 50 cents a gallon then). We had some good times just being ourselves, and we didn't always party. We met so many people out on 'the cruise' having good times and talking with people from the other high schools. There were so many people to meet.

One time we went to University of California, Santa Barbara to a concert to hear the Beach Boys, The Allman Brothers, Little Feat and other bands. We stopped at Jack in the Box for burgers to eat on during the day at the concert. The place was packed and we had a great time meeting other people. That was an all-day concert on the lawn and so much fun! There were hundreds of people scattered all over the lawn soaking up the tunes and the rays from the sun. We were just your average teenage California girls living on the coast enjoying life. I loved doing things with my friends and we always tried to keep busy.

Madonna Inn

Chapter 3

STRUGGLING TO WAKE UP

During the summer of 1975, we met two guys named Chuck and Bruce while we were playing frisbee at Waller Park. They asked if they could join in with us, no problem (we were 16 going on 17 and they were 19). So, we became friends with them. They were super nice guys, not to mention they were good looking. We met lots of people while playing frisbee or just walking around the park on our Sunday adventures. When we weren't at the beaches, we would hang out at Waller Park.

Two of my friends got part time jobs working at Sears while I babysat the kids next door or other neighborhood kids. The first semester of my senior year, I ended up having to take two night classes in order to get extra credits to graduate. (Because I ditched school so much and failed a couple of classes, that was my 'punishment').

One of those classes required me to volunteer, so one of my classmates and I volunteered at the local Planned Parenthood for two months. We were required to work one night a week in the lab. I didn't think much about it, all I knew at the time was that underage girls could get pregnancy tests, birth control or be checked for STDs there. (I worked in the lab doing the pregnancy testing). We really didn't think much about what was going on at PP, but I did notice several girls came in more than once during my semester. Debbie and I completed our volunteer time, we passed our class and started the second semester of our senior year.

My two friends who were working part time, graduated early from high school. They had goals and dreams they wanted to reach. That left me to my own devices without my friends to run with. I attended four classes instead of a full schedule for the rest of my senior year in 1976. Plus, I babysat the kids next door. I still didn't have any goals or dreams other than to leave home when I turned 18. I had no idea what I really wanted to do, other than to get out of the house.

One of the girls in my 'family' class asked me to go with her to Pismo Beach on a Friday night so we could just hang out and meet people. We ended up at a party where a bunch of older people were, most of them surfers. I drank a beer and observed the people around me. Patty met an older guy and started messing around with him, and that made me nervous. I was not into messing around with anyone. I just went to parties to hang out and meet people, smoke pot or drink beer, nothing else. I went with her a couple of times to party in Pismo on the weekends, but then I backed off because I didn't want a reputation like my friend.

I ran into Chuck a month later and he asked what I'd been up to, and I told him about my friend Patty. He ended up telling me that he and Patty had dated for a while and he hoped she didn't get pregnant again. And I thought to myself, "WHAT?" He told me that she'd had an abortion before they had broken up. I had no idea what to think about all of that. I liked Patty but she was a little too wild for me when it came to guys.

One Friday night, I ended up going to Pismo Beach with another friend to a party. I saw several people that I knew, and then ran into Patty. She wanted to talk with me outside. So, we went outside and she told me that Chuck had called her to let her know that he'd told me about her abortion. I found out that she really had dated Chuck for a while and that she had gotten pregnant. Patty told me that he talked her into having an abortion. Patty explained to me that she needed to have an abortion in order to finish high school without a baby. She explained that Chuck wasn't ready to settle down at all and didn't need a kid at that time in his life either. I just listened to her. However, I didn't say a word about anything because I was still clueless on what abortion really entailed. I didn't want to know the details. My conversation with Patty left me speechless and unsure of really what to think. I didn't sit in judgment of her, but I just wasn't sure how I felt about all of the information I was given to digest.

After talking with Patty, my other friend and I stayed at the party for a while. Then we decided to leave and went to hang out by the Pismo Pier to watch the waves and see if we would run into anyone we knew. That night was windy and cool but we didn't stay out too long before heading home.

Reflecting on my partying in Pismo, I decided that I really didn't need to be going to parties with so many older people. I was still underage and it wasn't that I didn't like being around older people, I just felt uncomfortable at times because I was still in high school. I also knew that many people were doing things I did not want to do. I liked meeting other people, but I knew these people were over my head and I wasn't willing to go there.

Chapter 4

SUE AND DAVE

The first week of May I ran into Chuck and he invited me to a huge party he was having on the 7th. He told me he had someone for me to meet. I said I would go if I could bring a friend of mine. Chuck told me that was okay. So, I called Audrey and talked her into going to this party with me.

We drove up to a ranch house and parked among many other vehicles in the dirt. There were SO many people at this party, and most of them were over 21. (We were still 17 and seniors in high school). So, I introduced Audrey to Chuck, and I was introduced to Dave. Wow. He was cute and a super nice guy. Dave was very easy to talk to. He'd recently turned 18 in April and worked in the body shop for a local car dealer, still living at home with his parents. We ended up talking most of the night, drinking beer and smoking pot.

After midnight most of the people left as the party was winding down. There were 6 of us left at the house still sitting around and talking. (Chuck lived with a married couple). As we were sitting around talking, some bikers showed up to ask about the party. Chuck's roommate told them to take a hike while showing his pistol (yep, freaked me out).

Later Dave and I went outside to talk and we got a blanket to lay on and look at the stars while we were talking about life and ourselves. He was such an easygoing nice guy and I already really liked him. We talked and laughed and he made me feel so relaxed. Then he asked me for my phone number and I wrote it down for him. (That was the beginning of our relationship). Then, Audrey and I finally left and headed home. We talked about Dave and Chuck, and we decided we both liked them.

Sunday came around and Dave took me to meet his family, I really liked them. We stayed at the house long enough for them to check me out, then we took off to go see some friends. I waited two weeks before I took him to meet my parents. My dad wasn't the greatest to be around at that time.

I usually went to Dave's house with him, or we would drive around by the beaches, Colson Canyon, San Luis Obispo or Waller Park. We had so much fun driving around and hanging out with friends as well.

He also liked to take me to the A&W Root Beer on Broadway so we could park and eat our food at the outside stall. I loved the deep-fried burritos with taco sauce and mugs of cold A&W Root Beer! Dave even bought me a small glass mug to keep as a souvenir. Sometimes we'd just sit there, eat, talk and just watch other people for hours.

Dave was silly at times. We would be driving down the road with the windows down and music blaring on his stereo. Dave singing at the top of his lungs. He was always singing to me, usually singing "Baby I Love Your Way" by Peter Frampton, "Let It Grow" by Eric Clapton, or "I'm Easy" by Keith Carradine. Our favorite besides Peter Frampton was Aerosmith and Eric Clapton. Sure enough, if we were listening to Aerosmith…the music was really loud!

One day we took Randy with us to Lake Marie Estates so the guys could skateboard on the hills in the neighborhood. Dave's car was a Ford Pinto with a 4 speed and he had me drive so he and Randy could hold onto the bumper. He'd tell me to drive fast and then stop quick so they could let go and take off down a hill. They were crazy funny, but there were times it scared me. I laughed so hard when they would skate past me, but I was afraid one of them would fall off and crash.

Sometimes we'd take friends with us and drive up to Colson Canyon just to goof off. Not really much to do except check out camp sites or drive on the dirt roads, maybe smoke some pot. It was nice and peaceful with all the oak trees. Sometimes we would see other people up there but not very often. One time we went there at night. It was very dark and eerie in places, but not too bad when the moon was full.

We also loved going to San Luis to walk up and down the streets. There was so much to see as the town was so beautiful and peaceful. The downtown shops were cool to check out, and the architecture was amazing. We would walk to the Mission just to look around or sit down to admire all the views around it. I absolutely loved spending time in San Luis. The older houses were pretty to look at as we drove around, as well as the surrounding countryside. The trees, flowers, palm trees, and everything made for a beautiful drive.

One day we found a little shop with trinkets, candles and different cards. That is where Dave found a card with a poem that he liked. When we got ready to head back down the road home, he gave me a card that had this poem written inside.

Love

by Roy Croft

I love you,
Not only for what you are,
But for what I am
When I am with you.

I love you,
Not only for what
You have made of yourself,
But for what
You are making of me.

I love you
For the part of me
That you bring out;
I love you
For putting your hand
Into my heaped-up heart
And passing over
All the foolish, weak things
That you can't help
Dimly seeing there,
And for drawing out
Into the light
All the beautiful belongings
That no one else had looked
Quite far enough to find.

I love you because you
Are helping me to make
Of the lumbar of my life
Not a tavern
But a temple;
Out of the works
Of my every day
Not a reproach
But a song.

I love you
Because you have done
More than any creed
Could have done
To make me good,
And more than any fate
Could have done
To make me happy.

You have done it
Without a touch,
Without a word,
Without a sign.
You have done it
By being yourself.
Perhaps that is what
Being a friend means,
After all.

Reading every line in this card touched my heart deeply. Dave told me that he loved me and could not imagine his life without me in it. I felt the same. He was so tenderhearted, and so very real.

One day Dave was excited because he found out the band "Thin Lizzy" was going to be in concert at the fairgrounds. Oh yeah, we decided to go, (tickets were $5 I think at that time) and we took along a friend of his with us. We were allowed to take a 6 pack of beer (crazy) into the building, and we smoked pot as well during that concert. We had so much fun! We all agreed, this was one of the best concerts we had ever been to.

Dave and I became very close (and yes, sexually involved as well) and we talked about everything. When he wasn't working and I wasn't babysitting, we were inseparable. He was easygoing, easy to talk with and we never got into any arguments. We were so different from our parents; we didn't yell or argue at all. Both of our fathers had the same personality traits, but my dad had big time anger issues. Both of our dad's had been in the military as well. Dave didn't need to do anything to impress me, and I didn't have to do anything to impress him. We had a very good relationship without any pretenses. We were just being ourselves. That is what I liked about him the most, I could be myself.

Unfortunately, my dad and I were not getting along, and it made me want to leave home even more. June 10, 1976 was my high school graduation. My dad was angry with me and refused to go. He said I didn't deserve to graduate because I had bad grades and no goals in life. I'm not kidding. However, I had gone to night school to obtain extra credits in order to graduate. It didn't make any difference to my dad that I had taken night school, I could not live up to his standards.

Dave and his family went to my graduation, my mom did as well. Before the ceremony, Dave and one of our other friends picked me up. We smoked some pot before I needed to meet my mom in the parking lot in order to get my graduation gown on. I wondered, would she be able to tell I was high?

What were we thinking? Other people we knew did the same thing, and my graduation ceremony was interesting to say the least. So many people were wasted, it was funny but sad really. (My high school class was very large). I have no idea how I walked across that stage. I even wore purple sunglasses to match my graduation gown. After the ceremony, Dave and I took off to celebrate.

Just a few days later on June 12th, I turned 18. Dave's parents had a beautiful bouquet of flowers delivered to me. Dave picked me up when he got off work to take me to his house. His parents gave me a birthstone ring for my birthday (Alexandrite), and they made shrimp cocktail for us before we headed to Pismo Beach.

Dave took me to Trader Nick's for my birthday dinner. We both had the Surf N Turf along with a bottle of Mateus wine (didn't they know we were only 18 years old?). We sat by the window that looked out at the ocean waves, and that is where he asked me to marry him. I was so excited! It didn't scare me or freak me out, it just felt right. So, I said yes!

After dinner, we drove to the pier at Pismo Beach and walked down to the sand. Listening to the waves of the ocean and walking barefoot in the sand, so calm and peaceful. The sound of the waves crashing was music to my ears. I love the beach and how it makes me feel! We may have been young and naive in many ways, but we knew we were meant for each other. Dave and his parents made my birthday amazing to say the least. It was a very good day.

One day Dave took me to AFCO to get me a three-tiered wooden plant stand and three plants. The planter was really cool looking and I couldn't wait to fix up my plants to set them in. He got me a Maidenhair fern, an arrowhead plant and a string of pearls succulent.

On the 4th of July, I was invited to go with Dave and his family to Lopez Lake, along with some neighbor friends of theirs. Dave was an excellent swimmer and he kept trying to get me into the lake water to swim. I was not having any of it! I could swim in the ocean but the lake scared me. I have no idea as to why but the feel of the icky sand of a lake bottom did not make me comfortable at all. I finally gave in and allowed Dave to coax me into the water. The water was warm but I didn't want my feet touching the bottom! We had such a fantastic day of BBQing and hanging out with Dave's family and their friends. I really liked being around Dave's family.

When the Santa Barbara County Fair started in July; Dave and I, along with Chuck and Audrey, went for the day and half the night. We had such a blast that day riding different rides and walking around. When we rode the 'swings' we all grabbed each other's pant legs to hold onto while up in the air. We were all laughing so hard the whole ride!

Audrey and I laughed so hard when the guys bought balloons and inhaled the helium, talking crazy! They sounded like chipmunks! I thought I would pass out from laughing so hard! Totally hilarious! They tried to get us to do it as well but we were not having it. We had so much fun. I never wanted the day to end. Dave had a pocket full of change and we ended up at the booth where you throw dimes for prizes. He was pretty good at it and I came home with quite a few glass kitchen items, including a glass carnival candy dish.

Trader Nicks

Senior Picture - 1976

Chapter 5

FINDING OUT I AM PREGNANT

At the end of July, I found out I was pregnant and freaked out. I never paid attention that I never had a period while we were dating. What were we thinking? That's just it. We hadn't been thinking. I went to Planned Parenthood for a pregnancy test but didn't want to talk about anything else other than yes it was positive. I told Dave and he kept telling me it would be okay, things would work out, and to stop worrying. We were planning on getting married anyway, just sooner than we planned. So, we decided to get married the weekend of Labor Day but kept it to ourselves.

I thought of the times I smoked pot, smoked cigarettes and drank beer while partying. My mind was reeling. Dave's mom lost a baby the previous year (or that year, I can't remember) and I could not talk to her about this. There was no way I was telling my parents. My mom lost a baby the year before I was born and had three miscarriages after me.

The more I thought about it, I couldn't even talk to Dave about the crazy thoughts in my head. Why was I so afraid to completely trust him with my fears and crazy thoughts? He started talking about baby names and if we had a boy, we should name him Richard Christopher. I was okay with that. What was wrong with me? I wanted to marry my boyfriend and have this baby. Yet, I still couldn't talk about my fears. We knew that we wanted to be married, but we never really talked about what that part of our future meant. How would we make it? Where would we live? His parents said we could live with them, but it made me a little nervous to think about that. I didn't think about continuing my education at the junior college, and the only 'jobs' I had were babysitting neighborhood kids. But Dave kept telling me everything would be okay.

One day I ended up going to Chuck's and talking to him about my pregnancy. What were Dave and I going to do? His roommates were home that day and they told me about their abortion experience. They all told me I needed to get a pregnancy test at Planned Parenthood. They also said I really needed to have an abortion because I had partied here and there quite a bit. I told them I already had a pregnancy test that was positive. Chuck and his roommates told me that my baby would be deformed because I had partied (I was not a heavy-duty party girl like other people I knew), that is why I needed to talk with Planned

Parenthood. I had no idea what an abortion was like and didn't know if I really wanted to do that.

My second visit with Planned Parenthood confirmed that yes, I was pregnant. I thought this was silly because, of course I was pregnant, this was my second positive test. They told me that my baby was a mass of cells and not a fetus. I was 12-16 weeks pregnant at the time. How could that be just a mass of cells? I believed what they told me because they were the experts right? They told me I needed an abortion and convinced me that an abortion was the ONLY choice I had. They told me it was my body, and my choice. That's what they tell you. That it is YOUR BODY, YOUR CHOICE.

I thought to myself, if I only had a mass of cells and not a real baby, why were they pushing me to have an abortion so strongly? They tell you it's a safe procedure, no big deal. But they kept trying to convince me that an abortion was my best and only real option. Why was this push for abortion so important from everyone, especially Planned Parenthood? I just couldn't understand why everyone kept pushing me to make this decision.

Pismo Beach

Chapter 6

THE FINAL DECISION

I thought about it for a couple of weeks, then I called and made an appointment for an abortion. I was so convinced that I was doing the right thing because people kept telling me that my baby would be damaged and not normal. How utterly sad that I could believe the lies I was fed. How brainwashed I was by Planned Parenthood, Chuck and his roommates. I was under so much pressure. Why was this the best thing for me to do? I felt like I had to, that there was no other way for me.

I could not even talk to Dave about my decision; he would never understand my fears. I don't even remember how Dave found out about the appointment for my abortion. That was our first argument. It was horrible. I'm pretty sure Chuck told him. Dave came over and took me to talk with his parents. They were furious and tried talking some sense into me. Why oh why did he make me go talk to them? Dave's mom told me about the baby she lost and about the second baby that she lost that year or the previous year, I don't remember. But it was very hard for her to even comprehend what I was thinking, and why I would make a decision to destroy a life inside of me. I was a wreck when we left his house.

I had to tell my parents, and that was even worse. My mom lost a baby before I was born and had 3 miscarriages after me. I was so overwhelmed I remember thinking I wanted to die. Before I knew it, Dave and his parents showed up at my house so we could all talk again. It was the most uncomfortable situation to say the least. So much tension, so much confusion. If Dave's dad had not threatened me with a lawyer to keep my baby, I would not have gone through with that appointment. I was the type of person when you threaten me, I would do the opposite and tell that person they were not in charge of me. I didn't like to be controlled; I would rebel.

That is when Dave and I were officially broken up. I was a mess. I wanted to die. Watching Dave and his parents leave my house was distressing. On the way out the front door, Dave turned around to look at me with such a sad face. How could I live without him in my life? Why was I so determined to destroy my child and my relationship with Dave? How could I let Planned Parenthood and others convince me that it's no big deal? Do I really know what I'm doing?
Chuck was supposed to take me to my appointment

the next day. My dad was so furious he told me to call Chuck and tell him he was NOT taking me to that appointment. So, I called Chuck and told him what was going on. My dad made my mom take me, and of all the people, she should not have.

I had to be in Santa Ynez at 6 a.m. for my procedure. Someone checked me in and I was taken to a room where I was given a hospital gown to put on. Then I was given some kind of medication by mouth before my procedure, and my vitals were taken. They told me that the pill was supposed to keep me calm and relaxed. I was a nervous wreck, but nobody was going to talk me out of doing this now. I was fully convinced that because it was my body and my choice. No clue as to what was really going to happen to me, nobody explained anything in depth.

A nurse finally came to get me and took me into the surgical room. I was put on a gurney, with my legs actually strapped in full leg stirrups that were straps of leather with heavy-duty buckles. I was given a shot in the cervix and I'm not sure how long it actually took before the procedure was started, but when the suction machine was turned on, it was loud. It reminded me of an air compressor in a car body shop.

At times, the noise was deafening to me. I was told that I would feel pressure but to lie still and not move at all. It seemed like forever before the procedure was over. So many thoughts were going through my mind. Then I started to feel what was happening inside of me. I felt the pulling and pressure, I started screaming and crying hysterically for them to stop. However, they wouldn't and couldn't stop the procedure. How could I put myself through this? They lied to me telling me, "It wasn't a big deal and I wouldn't feel anything." YES, I DID! I started to feel physically sick.

The doctor yelled for one of the nurses to hold me down and that my cervix/uterus could have been punctured. One nurse had to lay across me to keep me from moving. The other nurse made me hold and squeeze her hand to try to get me to calm down. She kept telling me that it was almost over and to be still. I was completely hysterical. Later my mom told me she could hear me screaming down the hall.

I thought to myself, "OH MY GOD! What have I done?" I was sobbing uncontrollably, my body was in shock and my mind was a mess. I thought I was going to die and my insides were all cut up. All I could think was, "Please make it stop!"

Finally, the procedure was over. I was hot, sweaty and shaking. They cleaned me up, unbuckled my legs from the straps and the stirrups were taken away. A nurse took me to my room and gave me something to calm me down.

Laying in a fetal position, all I could do was cry and say Dave's name over and over. I remember thinking, "What have I done to myself? Am I going to live or die?" All I could think about was Dave, what I'd done to myself, and what I'd done to him. How I had just destroyed a life inside of me.

I don't even remember getting dressed and getting into the car, but I remember we were close to Solvang. It sounds crazy, but I asked mom if she would take me to get a soft pretzel with cheese and a Coke. What the heck was wrong with me? I just committed murder by destroying the life that was inside of me. There's no way I had a mass of cells and it was not a fully developed baby. I was NOT in my right mind. Period. So, mom took me to get that pretzel and coke. As I sat and waited in the car, I knew I was out of my mind.

A couple of days later I was on the couch laying down. Mom was out running an errand at Sears. Sometime later I had gotten up to go to the bathroom and I completely freaked out because I had huge blood clots coming out of me. There was so much blood from hemorrhaging. I was crying and heard the phone ringing. I answered and it was my dad. All I could do was cry and he wanted to know what was wrong. Then he asked where my mom was but I couldn't remember. My mom came home and walked into the house. I handed her the phone and my dad told her what I'd told him. He told her to call the doctor immediately.

Mom made the call and was instructed to rush me back down to the hospital in Santa Ynez. I think she drove 80 miles per hour to get there. It turns out my cervix was not closing and I was rushed in. I was given an injection and medication to prevent an infection. I thought to myself, "Would my body ever be healed? Would my guilt destroy me as well?" I knew I needed to pull myself together.

A week later, I asked my mom to take me to get my long hair cut off, all of it off. Dave had loved my long hair. I wanted it gone. I had destroyed my baby and broken up with my boyfriend. I did not want a reminder. I felt so hollow inside, I wanted to die.

Chapter 7

THE EMOTIONAL WRECKAGE

It was August 22nd (Monday) and I just couldn't take it anymore. The voices in my head were making me crazy. I hated myself, my mind was a mess and I had no idea what I was going to do with my life. I called Audrey and told her I'd cut my hair off, that I killed my baby and I wanted to die because I couldn't take the guilt anymore. She told me to walk down to her house and she would call Dave. I told my mom I was going to see Audrey and I took off walking to her house. What was I going to do or say?

Dave was in the car waiting for me. We got into a huge argument. I got into his car and he told me to get out... nope, wasn't doing it. I reached over and locked my door, and he took off like a bat out of hell. That time I actually put my seatbelt on. I was scared to see him like that. He stopped and yelled at me to get out of the car, I told him NO. Then he took off again ended up at the house he had just moved into with a friend.

Randy and his dad were both at the house. When we walked in, Randy looked at me funny and Dave told him we were just going to talk. I gave Randy a crooked smile and shrugged my shoulders as I walked toward the bedroom. We went into Dave's room and we talked for a while and all I could do was cry. Then he called my house and told my dad that we were still going to get married. My dad didn't even say a word but he hung up on him. I ended up staying the night with Dave and he took me to his parents' house the next morning.

Dave's mom got in my face telling me she would never forgive me for what I did, and Dave's dad told her to shut up and never mention it again. It was a terrible scene, but I ended up staying there for two days. I was so uncomfortable that I ended up taking off on foot and ended up somewhere to call my mom to come get me. The guilt was eating me up inside and the way Dave's mom was so upset, totally unnerved me. I really couldn't blame her, but I couldn't take her condemnation.

My parents had no idea what to do with me. My mom ended up taking me to talk to some minister we didn't know. He suggested that they pack me up and have me go live with relatives out of state. Was there someone I could go stay with? What the heck was he talking about? I was sitting there numb, not knowing what to think or say. I couldn't even say anything, my mouth never opened.

So, we when we got back home, Mom called one of her sister's. She asked her if I could come and stay with her. Mom told my aunt everything that happened. But my aunt agreed and said I could come stay with them. I was packed up and we left for Texas early the next morning. Not. Telling. Anyone. Anything.

I kept wondering to myself, "Why was it best for me to pack up and leave? What was I supposed to do? Why didn't I stand up for myself? Why was this the best thing for me to do?" My mind was so messed up, I killed my baby by being talked into that abortion. I was also talked into walking out on my boyfriend and leaving my home state. More people convinced me it was all the right thing to do, that it was best for me.

Dave was the best thing that ever happened in my life. I loved him dearly. Why didn't we just sit down and talk about all my fears, why was I so convinced by others to make my decision? Why couldn't I just trust my boyfriend with everything, and why did I listen to others who really didn't have my best interest for me?

It was such a trying time in the early stages of Roe vs Wade. Feminists pushed for this, lived for this ruling. It was a woman's right as it was her body and her choice. What a disgusting lie, but I fell for it as well.

But I knew that I made a huge mistake that could not be corrected and undone. I was hopeless, defeated and scared out of my mind.

Now I'm packed up to do what? How do you heal your mind? How do you get past what you've done to yourself, your child and your boyfriend and your families? I was a total wreck inside my mind. I tried to pretend I was doing okay, but on the inside I really wasn't.

I remember thinking, "I cannot believe I'm leaving California. I'm leaving my friends behind. I'm leaving everything behind." I was very distraught and felt like I was in a fog. I kept wondering, "Will I ever be normal and feel like myself again? Where was that happy go-lucky girl that was so full of life? Where was the die-hard Sue who was the mouthy teenager that had been unafraid to speak her mind?"

The ride to Texas was not a fun one. I was so screwed up. I had no idea what I was supposed to do with my life.

Chapter 8

TEXAS

So unsure of myself and what is required of me on this journey. The ride to Texas was weird, just my mom and me. We ended up at my aunt's house Labor Day weekend, the weekend Dave and I planned to run off and get married. I ended up taking my mom to the airport in Shreveport, leaving the car with me while I'm in Texas.

I did not have contact with any of my friends or anyone back home in California. Nobody knew I'd left or where I was. Nobody really knew what I'd done, except for Dave and his parents, Chuck and his roommates, Audrey, and my parents.

Being in Texas, I only knew my relatives. I did not have any friends here and didn't really want to make any. This is not where I wanted to be. This was not where I belonged. Yes, I loved my family here, but I didn't want to live here.

My cousins from El Paso moved in with my grandparents and they were like younger sisters to me. I'm so thankful that I had them around. (They were in Oklahoma with my grandparents, while I was in Texas, only an hour away). I went there as much as I could until they moved to Texas close to me. My cousins and I were very close and I don't know what I'd done if they hadn't been around while I was here. They didn't really understand how messed up I was and all that I'd really been through. They only knew what I told them and I shrugged off the deep hurt inside of me and pretended I was the old me. As halfway to normal as I could be.

I still didn't have much self-esteem, goals or any dreams left inside me. I started writing poetry again here and there. I worked at Pizza Hut and helped open a new store for them but ended up quitting and started working at Dairy Queen. I never considered going to the local college to further my education, I had no idea what I was supposed to do with my life. I didn't want to be in Texas, yes, I loved my family but I was dying inside. I missed my friends, I missed the beaches, I missed Dave. I had contact with nobody back home.

My aunt took me to her church, and I attended Sunday school...but the teacher was an older man and the comments he made when looking at me. I knew that my aunt told him why I had moved to Texas. I was so upset that I called my mom to tell her and told her I would not go back to that church. That man made me feel condemned and dirty, unworthy.

I was too much of a California girl, and I felt that I did not fit in here in Texas. I dressed differently. I loved wearing my jeans and Dittos and did not dress up dressy unless I really wanted to. This girl was hip and more of a beach girl.

The end of November I met a really nice guy who was 21 and he asked me out. This guy was very nice and easy to talk to, someone I felt I could trust. When I brought him to the house to meet my aunt and uncle, they knew him and his family. Lovely.

We started talking more and he asked me what made me move in with my relatives, so I told him the whole story. Bad decision. We only had sex twice and that was only because I'd found out that Dave had a new girlfriend. I found out when I called to talk to him one night out of desperation. Randy was the one who told me. This guy I started seeing, I had trusted with my past in confidence. I had no idea he would later use this information against me. I was so utterly naive.

My aunt and I were not getting along, and one night she called my dad to come get this girl and take her back home.

So, I packed up and headed to Shreveport to pick my dad up at the airport. The look of disgust and anger was all over my dad's face, the drive back to California was silent. We drove straight through, only stopping for gas and to use the facilities. What a creepy ride back to California. I was extremely scared.

Scared of my dad. Scared to run into Dave. Scared to venture out in life. Scared to run into anyone.

What was I supposed to do with my life now? I hated the way I felt inside, hated the way my dad looked at me. So, what am I supposed to do when I get home?

San Luis Obispo Shops

Chapter 9

BACK IN CALIFORNIA

Being back home again was weird and I was such an emotional mess. However, I never let on to anyone that I was messed up on the inside. I was a good at pretending to be my old self. I got a job at the mall, but still didn't think about going back to school at the local junior college. I still had no hopes or dreams. I was just taking everything one day at a time. Linda, my best friend, moved back to the coast with her dad, in Nipomo, and we both worked at the same place in the mall.

At the end of January, mom took me to San Luis Obispo to hear a speaker named David Wilkerson, along with Dallas Holm and Praise. I'd seen the movie "The Cross and the Switchblade" and had also read the book. However, I'd never seen or heard David Wilkerson in person. The Holy Spirit started tugging on my heart during that service while Dallas Holm and his band were singing, but I ignored Him. Listening to David Wilkerson was amazing, but I couldn't make myself walk to the front to respond to the altar call.

I never had a menstrual cycle and I hid that fact for 4 months. I was so ashamed and never wanted to run into Chuck or Dave, let alone any of my friends. I sent a letter to the guy in Texas, he never acknowledged anything. I remember thinking, "Wow. What a fool I was."

My parents started going to church and my dad became born again. He gave up drinking and smoking cold turkey with no issues. What was going on? I'd never heard about being saved or born again. I grew up in the Methodist church. Yes, I knew all about Jesus dying on the cross and other religious facts but I don't remember ever hearing the story of salvation, or I didn't pay attention whenever I heard it preached at my grandparents' church in Oklahoma.

But I never knew what it was about to be "born again". I knew about "Jesus people" in school, we called them "Jesus Freaks". That was during the time of the Jesus movement when so many young people were getting saved.

I started going to church with my parents. On May 12, 1977 I accepted Jesus as my Lord and Savior. Pastor Smith and his family were from Australia and they welcomed me with open arms. The youth pastors, John and Pam, were also from Australia and they welcomed me with open arms as well. I am so very thankful for that leadership in my life. Everyone was amazing to that 18-year-old pregnant girl, which was so very needed. I was welcomed into the youth group and made many friends. I cannot explain how that time was so very needed and so very special for me.

I had my daughter that September, and the whole youth group showed up to see her. This baby was so loved, everybody wanted to hold her and they all passed her around to hold and love on. I was given 4 baby showers from different people, including my close friends, and that totally blew me away. My daughter's biological father to this day will not admit that she is his, and that's sad. Sad because I trusted someone with my darkest secret, sad that we didn't use protection and yet I was made out to be the lowest of low. I never asked for anything other than an admission of yes you were the one but I never got it. I was made out to be a liar and that hurt.

One Friday night I'd gone with a bunch of people from church to a local pizza place, taking my daughter with me. Across the room, I saw Randy with a bunch of people and he motioned for me to come over to talk with him. He started asking me questions. Where was I hiding out, and was that Dave's baby being passed around? I told him no she wasn't Dave's and asked him to never tell Dave that he'd seen me. I'd done my best to make myself hidden so I would never run into Dave and his new girlfriend. I was so ashamed and wanted to crawl into a hole and die. Ashamed because I aborted Dave's child, then became pregnant by someone who wanted nothing to do with me.

I remember thinking, "How could I have someone else's baby?" Randy begged me to meet with Dave and talk to him. I wondered why but I just didn't have it in me.

Days later, I got the phone call I truly dreaded. Could I meet with him and just talk? I finally agreed and took my friend Kelly with me. You could smell the drugs in the house, he wasn't the same. I wasn't the same. We were both still messed up from my former decision. I didn't stay long. I couldn't take the questions. I couldn't lie. I hated myself. I remember questioning, "How could God heal all the brokenness I created for the both of us?"

After that, I became part of a leadership training group with John and Pam leading us. I made good friends and learned much. I became good friends with Londa. But I knew there were many times she could not understand what I'd been through and why I was still messed up inside. Many times, she would listen to me and just pray and cry. Londa and her family were so good to me. I loved her family as my own. Her mom was so full of Godly wisdom, her dad was very loving and liked teasing me at times. So very thankful for all of them.

There was a split in my church and that was a mess for me to go through. I decided if Christians were going to act stupid, why be part of it? I needed to learn that we are all responsible for our actions. I also need to learn that Christians are not perfect and we are all guilty of sin. I had no idea what to think about it all. Certainly, I wasn't perfect but I did not agree with what happened.

Later we started going to the church that our former pastor started. So many people from the split were attending there. One night at church a movie was being shown about abortion. I tried to sit and watch, but when the sound of the suction machine started, I ran out crying hysterical. I never talked to anyone about my abortion before. Pam talked with me, Londa talked with me. I was still a mess inside. How could God heal that part of my life when I could not talk about it? Didn't want to talk and tried to ignore that part of my life.

My daughter and I moved out on our own, and I started going to business college. The little place I lived in was behind an elderly couple, and later my daughter and I called it 'the dirt roadhouse'. While in business college, I hooked up with a former friend I knew from school and I decided that I was done with church for a while.

I started going out dancing at clubs and being rebellious. I made sure I did not do anything crazy around my daughter, even though I knew I wasn't living right. Going out with friends was so much fun in San Luis or Santa Maria. I made more friends while I was attending business college. I tried going to church here and there at another location and made friends easily. Many times, I felt that I just didn't fit in, which was not really true. Why was I feeling this way? It was my self-confidence that was lacking, and yet guilt was tearing me up. I finished business college and started working. I was on my way in life! I was officially working and making my own money. I was a happy girl.

Solvang, California

Chapter 10

UPS AND DOWNS

I started going to church on the north end of town and made friends. I still tried to fit in. I tried to be a Christian, I always thought about God but so many times the roller coaster ride in life was my new normal. The enemy (Satan) played with my mind over and over...I wasn't good enough to fit it, I'm a lousy Christian, nobody will ever accept you for who you are, etc.

Many times, I'd sit and write letters to God, poetry, and about things I was going through. It's not that I didn't believe God or believe his written word, I didn't believe in myself and had no idea how I could be an overcomer in life. My self-esteem was not that great, I still had suppressed hurt pushed down to the bottom of my core being.

There were times I felt like if I died, everyone would be better off without me on this earth. However, that was only a thought. I watched other people around me, how they were so quickly accepted by people, and I was on the outside looking in. Why couldn't people accept me for who I was? I was outspoken and told it like it was, not pretentious at all.

I watched those who were pretentious, and they were accepted quickly. Why? I was not mean or callous, but if you asked my opinion, I told you. I wasn't the type to butter people up to be accepted. I watched those who 'worked' people and it churned my insides to see what was going on. (Later on, I learned this is the spirit of Jezebel).

I felt 'less than' when I was around people at church. There were times I knew people were watching, and knew I wasn't living right, yet I felt judged and sentenced as unworthy. Did those people ever pray for me? Those people didn't try to really get to know me at all, they just knew who I was.

How could God ever truly forgive me? Why do I continue to have the highs and lows in life when I really wanted a true fruitful Christian life? My self-esteem was so lacking. It was hard for me to pray and believe so many times. Yet, God brought so many different people in my life who needed to be encouraged or have someone listen to them. I always tried to help others.

I had no idea that God would free me and use those places of difficulty that I'd gone through to help others. How God healed me of those places, to help other people.

Yet there were people who were speaking into my life regarding all of this. Telling me that God wanted to use me, that the reason I went through such difficult places in my life was the very thing He wanted to use to help other people. I wondered, "Could He do that? Did He really want to use me to help other people?" YES, He did.

Shell Beach

Chapter 11

GOD HAS A PLAN AND PURPOSE FOR ME

My walk with God had so many ups and downs. I just could not understand why God loved me so much and wanted to see me whole. In the 1990's we had so many prophetic people come to our church in Santa Maria. People like Kim Clement, Bill Hamon, Dutch Sheets, John Cain, Bob Jones, and many others. I sat in so many of those meetings to learn. The prophetic conferences were amazing, I never truly knew about or understood this gift, until this time in my life. I soaked it all in.

One day in 1993, I felt God tugging on my heart to go home at lunch, to call information in Arizona, to find Dave. I did. All I could do was cry and beg for forgiveness, which I got from him. We kept in touch for a couple of weeks, then one day I got a call from a friend of his, telling me that Dave got back into drugs and was on the streets. I was shocked.

Moving forward with life. I tried to be a good mom to both of my daughters while they were growing up. I'm not perfect but I did the best I could. I tried to trust God but could never understand why I was still such a mess on the inside.

2002 came along and my parents sold their house to relocate to Texas. (long story). My youngest daughter and I came with them. Thing is, I had an amazing job in Santa Barbara, and I had to leave.

I was still angry with God and tried going to church here and there but just could not get it together. I still felt like I didn't fit in and really, I was mad at God for many reasons.

In 2012, I left for a job in Nashville, TN. I was traveling and making very good money. This job was amazing and they paid for all my expenses and even my apartment. There was so much to learn and so much to see!

Being in Tennessee was awesome! There was so much history. I realized how much I took for granted with history classes in school by not paying attention. I went sightseeing to different plantations, confederate cemeteries and just driving around to different places looking at houses, and all kinds of other fun things. I love the beaches back home, but there was something about being in Tennessee that truly amazed me.

I was supposed to fly home for Thanksgiving that year, but that Monday a friend of mine drove by my house in Texarkana at 6:30 am and saw an ambulance there. She called to tell me and wanted to know what was going on. I had no idea. I tried calling my family members to find out but couldn't get an answer from anyone. I went to work and talked to my director but she wouldn't let me leave when I wanted to. She instructed me to go home, relax a bit and then call her when I was calm. She said she would then consider letting me drive home. I finished packing my car, still couldn't get hold of anyone at home, and my boss finally let me leave. That was a long, more than 7-hour trip driving back to Texarkana.

When I arrived, I found out that Mom had ended up in the hospital but they let her come home the next day. I watched my dad the rest of the week and I kept feeling something wasn't right. I left that Sunday to head back up to Nashville. That whole week I kept feeling like something still wasn't right. Thursday night I packed my car, typed up a letter of resignation and went to work that Friday morning and quit my job. I didn't tell my parents or anyone else that I was on my way back to Texas. I just left Tennessee and showed up at home in Texarkana.

Chapter 12

ANOTHER RECONNECTION WITH DAVE

That December in 2012 Dave and I reconnected. He's back on the coast and gotten his life back together after being homeless and on the streets doing drugs. He became involved in a church and had given his life to Christ. He'd also given his testimony at a couple of locations including a local college.

That was fabulous news! He told me about losing everything, about being on the streets on drugs, eating out of trash cans and hiding from police, etc. He would become an advocate for the homeless and people on drugs. He enjoyed helping people get their needs met and to encourage them all that he could.

We never talked about my abortion in depth, but there was continued healing when we did finally speak about it. I think Dave skirted around it on purpose, but he told me that he forgave me and held nothing against me. We never ever talked about anything regarding that abortion in depth. Not about the emotional scars, etc.

I started working out of town at a hospital for a former boss at the end of January 2013. The next month my dad was not doing well, and the home health nurse finally convinced him that I needed to take him to the walk-in clinic. The doctor there said my dad needed to be admitted to the hospital. I took him to the hospital while the doc wrote up the orders for admission and faxed it before I got there.

Dad needed blood work, a blood transfusion and bone marrow aspiration. He was diagnosed with MDS (myelodysplastic syndrome), which eventually and quickly turned into Leukemia. My dad was in the hospital for a couple of days, then released home with Home Health coming to the house.

Home health came in to take vitals, etc. for my dad, and they were amazing. In April we had 3 friends from California show up. I had no idea they were here until I pulled up in the driveway and saw Donna's van, and Sue sweeping the sidewalk. I was like, what is Sue doing here and where is everyone else?

I got out of the car, we hugged and I started blurting out about my past. I had never done that before. Where on earth was this coming from? I had no idea this would be the time for God to begin doing a work in me for inner healing, to get me ready for the place HE has for me to step into.

OHMYGOSH...WHY did I just blurt that all out? Because God wanted to heal that dark hidden suppressed hurt inside of me.

I could not believe that our friends showed up to help us out! God had a plan indeed. He sent us friends from back home, I call them our California Angels.

Susan at Shell Beach – 1975

Chapter 13

INNER HEALING BEGINS

Our California angels stayed with us for a month. It was Jesus every day in my parents' house. I never knew what I would walk into when I got home from work; someone on the floor face down praying, someone reading the bible to my dad, worship music playing.

One night my dad tried to tell my mom that he knew he was on death's doorstep, and she could not understand what he was saying.   asked him and he said he wanted to have communion. Mom called their pastor to come over, and then we called to have our next-door neighbor come to the house (he's an associate pastor of a local church). They both showed up and so did Jesus. My dad did not die that night.

On a Saturday, we planned on going to church and Ross was going to stay with my dad, but Ross said that he felt like we all needed to stay, he felt that God was going to do something. We had a CD playing that friends of ours recorded. There was a certain song playing and I asked someone to play it again. That song was so ministering.

My dad's hospital bed was in the front room. I was sitting on the couch by my dad when that song started playing again. He looked at me and said: "Sue, I want to make sure that we are good, that things between us are okay". I knew exactly what he was talking about. He was talking about me, Dave, and all that happened, he wanted to make sure we both forgave each other. I said yes, we were okay. All I could do was sob and cry, and he cried.

Days later Sue talked with me and asked me to come into the bedroom with her. She told me that I needed to forgive myself, forgive others and ask for forgiveness (the 3 forgiveness's). And then she walked me through deliverance healing. Peace that I hadn't had in 37 years was all over me. She also walked me through cutting soul ties. So much weight was lifted off me!

There were other opportunities with healing for me to walk through while they were here with us. I had divine appointments with the Holy Spirit for inner healing. I finally allowed God into those dark places to heal my past.

After our Angels left, my dad lived 3 more weeks. Dave and I reconnected in 2012 and the weird thing was, if

I ever had the radio on and I heard the song "Baby, I Love Your Way', I either got a call from Dave or I called him.

July 8, 2013, Dave called me and wanted to talk about the conversation he had with my dad in 1976 after I was packed up and on my way to Texas. He told me about that conversation in detail. I was shocked, angry and mostly disappointed. What the heck?

Talking to Dave here and there was healing for both of us, he never forgot the places we went to or the things we talked about. We still never talked in depth about that horrible hurt. The most important thing about us was the healing that God wanted to do in both of our lives. Not to get back together, but to be friends.

Sue & Audrey

Chapter 14

TWO DREAMS IN 2015

April 1, 2015 my long time very best friend, Linda Ruth, died from lung cancer. I was devastated to lose my sister. It had been so very long since I'd seen her in person and I was not able to go visit her before she died.

Ryan LeStrange was at a local church that night and the next 2 nights, but I could not go on April 1st because I was so very sad about losing my friend. Mom and I went the next night and God healed the muscle under my armpit. I had torn it while doing yard work months before. We started going to that church because I was sure that's where we needed to be at that time.

That summer I had 2 dreams in one week. One was about Cambria, the other about San Luis Obispo. I asked God, are you telling me I need to go back home to the coast? At the time, I was working at home doing medical billing for a company out of Dallas. So, I spoke to my director about going to California, and my boss told me, "Susan, home is anywhere as long as you are doing your job". Okay. Did not need to tell me twice.

So, I called bestie, Audrey, and told her about my dreams. She told me to come and stay with her. So, I talked to mom about it and that I was headed to California. Well, she ended up going with me and she stayed with our friend Donna for a month.

What was so cool was that we would show up to see people we knew, visited different churches so we could see people who knew us. I loved the ultimate surprise and the tears and laughter that followed.

During this time back on the central coast, God took me back to places and showed me where I previously learned from HIM. I reconnected with former classmates who had become Christians and had amazing conversations. I also needed healing from trauma and terror from a very bad car accident I had in 1991. My car had totaled about ¼ mile from where I was living. Flipped my car twice and before sitting upright. No seatbelt on.

Dave knew I was coming back to California, and suggested we meet up sometime during my stay. That never happened, and it is okay. I'm pretty sure we were not supposed to see each other in person.

I still needed to walk through inner healing, and that was part of God's plan. To continue the healing process in me, and for me to visit different churches with prophetic conferences, etc. God spoke into my life prophetically through many people while I was back home. Confirmation from prophetic words previously spoken over me.

Being near the beaches, walking on the sand and listening to the roar of the waves was so refreshing for me. I reflected on so many things in my life while at the beach. Home. The sounds, the scents, the peaceful feeling I had. I soaked it all in and I didn't want to go back to Texas.

Sue took me to eat at a restaurant in Avila Beach one day and we sat and talked for a long time. When we left the restaurant, we just walked up and down the sidewalks and along the sand. As we would talk and I would bring something up, she would ask me what God was showing me about that. So, I'd tell her. Then she would walk me through forgiveness, healing and deliverance.

I stayed with Audrey for 2 months, and then ended up on the property where Londa's dad lived in Nipomo for 2 and a half months. Londa and I went to prophetic conferences in Santa Maria, I received so many words spoken over me, and so much healing and encouragement.

God did so much for me during that time in California. Yet, He set it up to where I would have to go back to Texas. Believe me, I was not happy...period. I cried and begged God to let me stay, yet He had plans for me back in Texas.

One day after work I got in the car and drove to San Luis Obispo to drive around one more time. To soak in the beautiful scenery and trace back all my favorite places. I drove to my favorite beaches, cried and begged God to allow me to stay on the coast. I was not happy. Period. I called Linda's mom and talked with her, and she gave me the mom speech. Didn't I need to listen to God and what He wanted for me? Ouch.

Chapter 15

BACK ON THE ROAD TO TEXAS

The drive back to Texas was in February 2016. I'd never seen so many California poppies on the hills that looked completely orange in some places. I'd never seen the desert in bloom, and it was. My drive back was really awesome because God showed out with the beauty all around on my drive back to Texas. Once I finally got back home in Texas, it took me awhile to get over me, but I was so amazed at all God had done regarding inner healing and finally realizing that HE wants to use me.

Dave and I didn't talk too much during this year of 2016, just off and on like before. In 2017 he was going through a very tough time and I told him that he needed to set some boundaries with the person he was having a tough time with. Our last conversation was in March 2017. God told me to back off and let him go.

Starting in April 2017 was a difficulty. I lost 2 family members within 2 weeks (one was 62 and the other was 26), then I lost 4 school mates.

2:30 am on Father's Day, I woke up and grabbed my phone to look at my Facebook page, and the Santa Maria Times to check obituaries. (Yes, I did that here and there to keep tabs on my hometown deaths). The first obituary I saw was Dave's. He died 2 weeks previously. I was numb, in shock and couldn't think. I didn't cry. That week the more I thought about it, my emotions started playing with me. His death was so very emotionally hard for me.

I finally realized that between April and June I'd lost 7 people to death. Please God, not anymore.

After sending 2 messages through Facebook, I finally had someone reach out to me and was told that Dave died from an overdose. I was shocked and shaken to the core...God set him free from drugs and alcohol. Why?

During the day, I pretended to be okay, at night I would fall apart. Maybe deep down I thought we would eventually get back together. We also needed to talk in depth about everything; because that is something, we did not get to do.

Dave desperately needed inner healing regarding my abortion. The one thing that we truly experienced between us was total forgiveness, and that was a beginning of healing.

It took me about a year to get over the death of Dave, but still could not understand why I was having such a difficult time of letting go. One day I spoke with Sue about it and explained to her that I could not understand why I was still so distraught over Dave's death. I'd broken the soul ties, why was I emotionally distraught? After listening to me, Sue explained that I needed to cut the emotional ties as well. Okay, that made sense. So, I got myself alone with God and started praying, and breaking the emotional ties with Dave.

With all the pain, heartache and the yo-yo walk with God. I knew one day that my story would be shared when I was totally set free of the things that were still trying to hold me down.

Chapter 16

DEEPER STILL

In 2019, I decided that I wanted to volunteer at the local pregnancy center, so I contacted someone and submitted paperwork. It took a few months but I was finally approved and went about four times to learn the ropes and what they wanted me to do. I was also given a book and workbook about post-abortion healing and I put that in my basket at home with other books. I'd spoken to the volunteer coordinator and told her my story. Even though I'd walked through healing and deliverance over my past abortion, I knew I still had 'residue' that God wanted to bring out for my final healing.

During that short time of volunteering, I began to feel like I needed to back off and that God was directing me to hold off at the time. A couple of weeks later, I was contacted by the Director of the pregnancy center about the Deeper Still ministry for post-abortion healing. She asked if I would be interested? I asked for information and sent an email to Lori about attending a weekend session.

Due to circumstances beyond our control, the weekend session in April for the Deeper Still retreat was put off until the third week of June. I took off work that Friday and headed up to North Central Arkansas to the most amazing place for this 'adventure'. I was so in awe of the surrounding beauty of this place! I was greeted by a volunteer who took my suitcase and helped me unload my car. I was then greeted and checked in by a wonderful couple and met other volunteers as well. I was a bit early as my drive was over 4 hours. My stuff was taken to my room for me, and there were lots of goodies on a table for me to have if I wanted anything.

Other people began to arrive, and there ended up being 6 of us total who would participate in this retreat. I was so amazed by the volunteers and how they were there to serve us with whatever we needed. These volunteers are the true meaning of servants of Jesus. We ate together for meals, we had different sessions that we attended and met together for prayer. I don't want to go into detail, but I just want to say, the steps I went through at different sessions were exactly what I needed for my total breakthrough.

There were 2 times I had a very hard time. At one point I did not think I could go through with one session that I needed to do. I broke down and cried but I finally pushed through.What I do want to say is this, the Deeper Still team wants to make sure you have a relationship with Jesus, and that is very important, as well as see you walk in forgiveness and healing.

This was a much-needed healing experience for me so that I could allow God to heal the residue in my life regarding my past abortion. I cannot explain how FREE I feel inside! Now I can step into the destiny and calling I have over my life. I could not even get past the first 8 pages of my book that I wanted to write, and now I have much to say!

When I left the retreat to head home it was hot and muggy. The weather had been rainy and then sunny in different places. On my drive, I was listening to a song by Bethel Music called "The War Is Over". As I listened to the words and sang along, I played it over and over again and just listened. I remember thinking, "Oh WOW, play it again!" The lyrics of the song start out and they say, "The war is over, turn around. Lay your weapons on the ground." I listened again and I shouted, "YES, YES, YES! My war is over!" I laid my weapons down with forgiveness, and I knew that my final stage of total and complete healing and recovery had finally taken place. I had now finally let go of all of the guilt and shame regarding my past abortion. WHAT A WEEKEND FOR ME! WHAT FREEDOM!

So, while I was listening to this song, I looked to the left of my windshield at the clouds. I wish I could draw for you what I'd actually seen. The clouds were formed like God had shaped them just for me. The cloud formation was in the shape of a man from the chest up, holding a laughing baby cradled in his arms. The baby was smiling up into his face with one leg draped over his arm, and the other leg kicking up. One arm of the baby was raised toward the man's face reaching up. This is what God showed me in those clouds and He said to me, "Your baby is in the arms of his Father, safe and secure. I was so in awe at what I'd seen in that formation, and it totally blew me away! This is how much God loves me and He wanted to show me and tell me what I needed to hear for confirmation from that weekend.

God did so much for me during the Deeper Still retreat. I'm so very thankful I was pointed their way for my final healing. I have much to say and a story to write. I did have a title for the book I'm writing, but after my retreat I changed the title to "Breakthrough of Hope: My Story of Healing After Abortion".

When someone makes a decision to have an abortion, they do not realize how this decision affects others in their life, not to mention their own. For me, I was talked into my decision when Roe vs Wade was three years in the making. By reading my story you will understand what I am talking about. It is so very important not to judge someone by not understanding what that person has gone through or why they may do crazy things in their life. There are many people who need healing when it comes to abortion, if they seek for it. People in the church may not know about the past of someone yet they sit in judgment because they watch how they are walking with God or trying to. Yet those people don't need judgment, they need inner healing and prayer.

I have so much more to say but I will just say this, to the volunteers and coordinators of the Deeper Still ministry team, I cannot thank you enough for your ministry. This is so vitally needed and has been needed for many years. I am so very thankful for the ministry team of volunteers for my retreat weekend. Thank you for being true servants of Jesus, for serving us, being there for us, and walking us through the steps of healing so we can move forward in our walk with Christ. I love you all. I am so truly blessed by my experience and your love for us all. I am still totally blown away by God's amazing grace and love!

Colson Canyon La Brea Road Sign

Letter To Dave

Dave,

You are no longer on this earth and it saddens me to know that you are no longer here. I was shocked to find out how you left this world, and I will never understand. I thought I would fold up and die when I saw the newspaper with your obituary in it. I didn't think, I didn't feel, I didn't cry.

I'm so very thankful that God allowed forgiveness between you and I regarding the past. Thankful for not reconnecting once, but twice to begin our healing.

Knowing you and loving you was the best part of my life when we were together. I will never forget the times we went to the beach and walked along the sand, drove up to Colson Canyon and all the other places we hung out at. I loved your smile and how you would be silly and sing your songs to me while driving in your car. You were such a gentle soul who was genuine and real.

I'm so thankful that you were the one who truly loved me and allowed me to be me. I have never found that again with anyone else.

It's so sad that you never truly healed from the decision I made in aborting our child. Nobody knows or truly understands the hurt you go through emotionally. How you suppress that hurt deep down in your innermost being. How making unrealistic decisions in life is because of that hurt that never truly healed. It's sad that other people get hurt because of the choices we make in life. You so desperately needed inner healing.

I'm so sorry you never got to write your book, how you so desperately wanted others to read about your life. You may not have written your book, but you were able to share your personal story with so many people. You truly did make a difference for others.

I am truly hoping that by me telling our story, others will reach out for healing. That people will understand the hurt. Understand how abortion destroys lives, affects others in their circle around them. It causes so much emotional pain.

I am so thankful that God allowed me to be free from the hurt in my past, that HE showed me that our child is in your arms. I had to let you go in order to be free, but I will never forget the love that we shared.

Sue

Grief, after the initial shock of loss, comes in waves. When you're driving alone in your car, while you're doing the dishes, while you are getting ready for work, all of a sudden it hits you – how so very much you miss someone, and your breath catches, and your tears flow, and the sadness is so great that it's physically painful. I thought of you today, but that is nothing new. I thought about you yesterday and days before that too. I think of you in silence, I often speak your name. All I have are memories and our picture in a frame. Your memory is a keepsake from which I'll never part. God have you in His arms, I have you in my heart.

Letter To
My Unborn Son,
Richard Christopher

When I found out that you were growing inside of me, I was happy and scared. Your father felt the same. What were we going to do? What kind of parents would we be? What would you look like? Your dad came up with your name, and I agreed that it was a good name.

There were times I thought I could see your face, what you would actually look like when you were born. But I never gave you that chance. Little did I know that you were already formed, moving inside of me. It was such a difficult time all around us.

I was young and listened to other voices that convinced me that you were nothing more than a mass of cells. I'm so sorry I believed the lies. I had no idea that you would suffer so much pain, not realizing how I would suffer with physical and mental anguish myself afterward.

By making the decision I made; I never got to feel you growing inside of me. Never experienced birthing you or holding you as I looked into your face. I never gave any of your grandparents the experience of enjoying their first grandchild, you.

It took me years to find true healing and forgiveness for my choice, but I did. Your father and I reconnected and we began our healing process, and I'm so very thankful for that.

I know you are with other children who died the same way, and you are in the presence of God as one of HIS little angels. I am so very sorry little one that I didn't choose to have you, allowing you to grow up as you should have.

One day I will be able to see you, and I know you are in the arms of your father, for that I am thankful.

I love you,

Your Mom, Susan

. . . .

Psalm 139:13, For you formed my inward part, you wove me in my mother's womb.

. . . .

Resources

ABOUT PLANNED PARENTHOOD

Planned Parenthood traces its beginnings to the birth control movement led by Margaret Sanger and her colleagues, who opened the nation's first birth control clinic in 1916 in a poverty-stricken neighborhood of Brooklyn, New York. Created to free women from the "chronic condition" of pregnancy and the dangers of self-induced abortion, the clinic was shut down by police after only 10 days. Sanger and the others were imprisoned for violating the anti-obscenity Comstock Act of 1873. Sanger's continuing efforts led to the foundation of both the American Birth Control League in 1921 and the Birth Control Federation of America in 1939, which became Planned Parenthood in 1942.

Acutely aware of the issue of privacy related to women's reproductive freedom, Planned Parenthood was a plaintiff in *Griswold* v. *State of Connecticut* (1965), in which the Supreme Court recognized the right of married couples to use contraception, and it joined the grassroots movement to legalize abortion, which culminated in the court's historic ruling in *Roe* v. *Wade* (1973). Following the latter decision, Planned Parenthood and its local affiliates were involved in several legal suits concerning the issue of access to abortion, notably *Planned Parenthood of Southeastern Pennsylvania* v. *Casey* (1992), in which the Supreme Court upheld *Roe* v. *Wade* and established the principle that states may not place an "undue burden" on a woman's ability to obtain an abortion. The undue burden standard itself was reaffirmed by the court in *Whole Woman's Health* v. *Hellerstedt* (2016).

There is so much more regarding Planned Parenthood, too much to list here.

Now let me tell you this:
Roe vs Wade was 3 years in the making for legalized abortions when I had my abortion in 1976. What Planned Parenthood did for me was provide the pregnancy testing and pushed abortion as my only option.

They say they offer counseling. What kind of counseling they have other than for birth control is beyond me. There is no post-abortive counseling of any kind offered by them, why would they? They are out to make the big bucks by convincing teens/women to abort their children.

Planned Parenthood is in the money-making business, as they sell various parts of the baby for different prices. This industry needs to be shut down, period.

Sin destroys. It is no respecter of person or age, or what you have done. Sin is sin, there is no little or big sin. God forgives if you seek HIM.

MY THOUGHTS ON ABORTION

You are not GOD. It's not YOUR BODY because there is a body inside of your body. That body inside of you is a baby, not a mass of cells. For you to play God and decide to murder your child, yes abortion is murder, it is wrong. You cannot candy coat the decision of abortion as morally right. It's wrong. Abortion stops a beating heart, cuts a baby to pieces and destroys that life.

Abortion causes depression, PTSD, lack of self-esteem, guilt, thoughts of suicide, etc. It did for me. It is so destructive all around. Anyone who tries to convince you it's no big deal, they are liars or they have no conscience.

For me, even though I became a Christian, I struggled with my walk with God for many years. I suppressed the guilt and turmoil so deep inside myself that I was not aware of 'why' I did the things I did in life. Subconsciously I was trying to fill the void of pregnancy I ended and the boyfriend I walked out on. I tried to find happiness by partying, spending money on things I didn't need, or doing crazy things nobody could understand...never reaching down to heal that part of my life until it was God's timing for me.

For men that were part of the decision making for an abortion, or unaware that their partner had an abortion until after the fact. There needs to be inner healing as well. I know that if Dave realized he needed inner healing, and reached out for help, from the pain and hurt caused by me, he would not have done the things he did with drugs and alcohol.

For those of you who observe other Christians you know in your church or as your friends...if those people are struggling in their walk with God, ask God what they have been through and how you can pray for them. Don't sit and judge those people for the things they do or don't do, you have no idea what people have been through in life.

I do believe that because of the devastation of abortion, the circle of people that this act affects is also an area that needs inner healing and forgiveness. I had no idea how hurt my friend Audrey was, until I went to stay with her in California in 2015. Hurt because she had no idea, I would abort my baby, hurt because I packed up and left for Texas without telling her. Hurt because she was left to try and answer the questions Dave required of her and not having any answers for him or herself.

There are so many hurting people who need Jesus to forgive them, to let them know that they are forgiven, and they need to move forward. Step out of the comfort zone let God touch those areas and release the hurt and anger. I never knew there was help of any kind regarding everything I went through, I didn't realize how much I suppressed down in the depths of my being and held onto that hurt for so long.

Something else I recently learned is that abortion creates trauma. Post-Abortion Syndrome (PAS) is the condition occurring in both men and women after the abortion experience due to unresolved psychological and spiritual issues.

PAS is actually a form of Post-Traumatic Stress Disorder, a commonly recognized condition that often follows traumatizing events such as witnessing an act of violence or experiencing a natural disaster. Patterns of long-term emotional disorder include: depression, grief, anxiety, helplessness, despair, sorrow, lowered self-esteem, distrust, hostility, dependency on alcohol/chemicals/food/work, guilt, sexuality problems, self-condemnation, weeping, emptiness, distrust, frustration, insomnia, nightmares, dysfunctional relationships, flashbacks, anger, fear of rejection, bitterness, unforgiveness, fear of commitment, and the inability to form close relationships. (This information came from Heartbeat International)

TO THOSE OF YOU WHO HAVE GONE THROUGH AN ABORTION

Because I had an abortion, my past has not defined me, destroyed me, deterred me, or defeated me. It has only strengthened me because God set me free and healed me. I am now honestly and completely free from the personal decisions in my past and all the dark times I have gone through. It was not an easy road for me but I want you to know there is freedom for you as well. Never be a prisoner of your past. What you have gone through was a lesson, not a life sentence.

Above all, seek help for inner healing. If you became a Christian after having an abortion in your past, please do not allow the enemy (Satan) to torment you mentally any longer. Ask God for forgiveness and forgive yourself. Sometimes it is so very hard to understand how we can even forgive ourselves for the past. Do not give the enemy a foothold any longer. Seek inner healing, forgiveness and deliverance.

If you are not a Christian, just know that God loves you and is waiting for an invitation from you to invite Him into your life. There is no other way you can be completely free without Jesus; trust me, I know. You are someone to Jesus. He has a plan and a purpose for your life. Trust in Him and ask for dreams and visions to help you have peace and true inner healing. Get into God's Word and study all you can.

Forgive yourself. Don't wait as long as I did to finally allow God in those dark, suppressed places of hurt and despair. No longer allow the enemy to cut you asunder, stand firm and be free!

Don't let fear and intimidation take over your mind. Ask God to give you a renewed mind and a clean heart. Run after God with everything you have inside of you!

SCRIPTURES FOR REFLECTION:

Deuteronomy 31:8, "And the Lord is the one who goes ahead of you; He will be with you, He will not fail you or forsake you. Do not fear or be dismayed."

Colossians 3:1-3, "Therefore if you have been raised up with Christ, keep seeking the things above, where Christ is, seated at

the right hand of God. Set your mind on
the things above, not on the things that are
on earth. For you have died and your life is
hidden with Christ in God."

Proverbs 3:5-6, "Trust in the Lord with
all your heart and lean not on your own
understanding; in all your ways acknowledge
Him, and He will make your paths straight."

Psalm 103:8, "The Lord is compassionate
and gracious; slow to anger and abounding in
steadfast love."

RESOURCES TO CONSIDER FOR POST-ABORTION HEALING:

Deeper Still: This ministry hosts weekend healing retreats for both women and men who have experienced or participated in an abortion as the mother or father of the child. They hold 3 retreats a year plus a Chinese retreat at our homebase in Knoxville, TN as well as retreats happening around the country in the 20 different Deeper Still chapters! Enjoy looking around the website and please feel free to contact them with any questions you may have through info@GoDeeperStill.org.

Project Rachel: This website offers many helpful resources for those seeking post-abortion healing. Their website is Hopeafterabortion.org

There are many places to reach out for help and healing, seek God and research as to where you should find that help. Look for someone you can trust in ministry for true healing, but search and find that healing in your life.

A Note of Thanks

Thank you, Jesus for forgiveness, thank you for healing, thank you for opening doors for those who need emotional healing and deliverance. Thank you, God for restoration.

Psalm 46:1-2, God is our refuge and strength, a very present help in trouble. Therefore, we will not fear, though the earth be removed, and though the mountains be carried into the midst of the sea.

There are so many people who have spoken into my life, and I just want to say you mean the world to me.

Thank you to Pastor Smith and his family for loving me into the Kingdom.

Thank you to Pastor John Buesnel (and Pam) for loving me as a young pregnant teen

Thank you, Audrey, for being my lifelong die-hard best friend and sister.

Thank you, Londa and John, for being in my life for so long. Londa, you are my other bestie and lifelong friend who I call sister as well.

Thank you, Cee and Alan Teixiera, for listening to my story and being part of my 'family', encouraging me to 'Step Out' - here is my first major step.

Thank you to my California Angels: Sue, Ross, and Donna. You are my family as well.

Thank you, Sue, for mentoring me, being obedient in all things and being that Godly example. Thank you for walking me through those places that God wanted to heal.

Thank you to my parents for loving me and forgiving me.

So very thankful for so many people I know and love from my hometown churches who are 'family'. I love you all!

A&W Rootbeer Santa Maria California 1970's

AFCO Department Store Doubles Selling Space in New Store

AFCO – Our local department store

Avila Beach 1970's

CPSIA information can be obtained
at www.ICGtesting.com
Printed in the USA
BVHW071454210721
612518BV00017B/479